DAVID

THANK... _____ FOR
YOUR SUPPORT FOR
DR. VON HOFF. WHERE
HOPE EXISTS... ANYTHING
IS POSSIBLE! HOPE
YOU ENJOY!

REAL
HOPE

HAVE A
GREAT NEW YEAR!

BEST

THOSE EXISTS... ANYTHING

REAL
HOPE

How Hope Drives Positive Actions That Lead to Business, Leadership, and Real-World Victory

RANDY DOBBS
and
DR. RICHARD K. NONGARD

First Printing: November 2019

ISBN: 9781704841960

Dr. Richard K. Nongard

Expert Leadership Performance, LLC

15560 N. Frank L. Wright Blvd. B4-118

Scottsdale, AZ 85260

(702) 418-3332

www.Nongard.com

www.DobbsLeadership.com

CEO Randy Dobbs and Dr. Richard Nongard are available to speak at your event on a variety of topics.

Contents

About Randy Dobbs

RANDY DOBBS rose to become a CEO in a General Electric Company business with the encouragement and coaching of high-level executives including legendary General Electric Chairman Jack Welch. In a string of GE positions of increasing responsibility, Dobbs excelled as a turnaround specialist who transformed every organization he led and established a winning record of improved earnings. More recently, Dobbs used the same "secret sauce" to transform and improve earnings as CEO of Phillips Medical Systems, North America, and USIS, a leading global security service provider, where he led 7,000 knowledgeable workers to a new understanding of how to work together to achieve business results. Dobbs is now a Senior Operating Executive at Welsh, Carson, Anderson & Stowe, one of North America's most successful private equity firms. Mr. Dobbs is available to help your organization, large or small, create success. He is an author, a frequent keynote and motivational speaker, and he provides operational consulting services to both public and private companies. His book *Transformational Leadership: A Blueprint for*

Organizational Change has become a leadership bestseller. He is an expert in mentoring and coaching senior executives and is available to be on the board or serve as board chairman for your company. Additionally, he can serve as interim leader, assisting your company in high level executive search and to provide leadership during periods of transition or turnaround.

Contact Mr. Randy Dobbs at (703) 477-5803 or visit his website at www.DobbsLeadership.com.

Access the Real Hope Resources at www.RealHopeBook.com including Randy Dobbs TEDx presentation.

About Dr. Richard K. Nongard

DR. RICHARD NONGARD is a popular conference and keynote speaker, known for his relaxed and engaging style. His focus is on real-world solutions based on the science of leadership. His presentations focus on leadership, engagement and actionable strategies for business success. He holds a Doctorate in Transformational Leadership (Cultural Transformation) from Bakke Graduate University.

He is the Chairman of the Board for Best Buddies Nevada, Inc.

Richard is a business expert who started his career in 1983 as a cold-calling salesperson in the auto industry. He has excelled in both medical and educational sales, administration, and product development positions. Richard is a serial entrepreneur who has owned successful business ventures over the years.

Richard is the author of numerous books, publications, and training videos. His book on leadership, *Viral Leadership: How to Seize the Power of Now to Create Lasting Transformation in Business*, has already become a popular resource for leadership development. He has written many other books as well, including psychology textbooks that have been adapted as textbooks at the university level, and his 5-star reviews are a testament to the value Richard provides in both written and spoken media.

Dr. Richard K. Nongard is a coach, consultant and lecturer, offering services to business groups, sales groups and healthcare organizations. You can bring him to your organization to train your executives or front-line employees in Viral Leadership, Appreciative Inquiry and/or Multiple Intelligences.

To bring Dr. Richard K. Nongard to your organization or conference as a keynote speaker contact him at NONGARD.COM or (702) 418-3332.

Access the Real Hope Resources at www.RealHopeBook.com, including both Randy Dobbs and Richard Nongard's TEDx Presentations.

What People Are Saying About Real Hope

"Dobbs & Nongard know that when hope overcomes fear we can take the necessary actions that lead to success in personal life and business. Hope gave me the confidence to take the risks to start my business. Read this book to discover how hope as a strategy can work for you."

— Patrick J. Welsh, Co-founder,
Welsh, Carson, Anderson & Stowe

"Dobbs and Nongard understand how hope is transformational and share their insights for taking action on hope in a powerful way."

— Adam Johnson, Executive Director,
Democracy Prep at the Agassi Campus

"In my non-profit work, I have seen firsthand that hope changes lives. It changes people. It changes communities. Dobbs and Nongard show leaders effective ways to utilize hope as a strategy to make a difference in the world."

— Charlene Blackstone, State Director,
Best Buddies International Inc.

Foreword

By Victoria M Gallagher

TAKE A DEEP breath right now. Allow your mind to wander back to a moment when you had a burning desire within. Maybe you were a child. Perhaps that desire is still alive within you right now.

What is the one thing that determines whether you will take that desire and manifest it into reality?

How is it that a person can endure failure upon disappointment for years on end, yet continue to elicit from themselves relentless and sustainable perseverance to continue to pursue their desire?

It comes down to the choice one makes about that desire. Do you believe it's possible for you to achieve it? What is it that gives us that belief, that our desire is even possible when there is not even a shred of personal experience to back up our decision?

I didn't come this far to only come this far.

In the summer of 1999, shortly after becoming fully certified as a Hypnotherapist, I applied for a business license to start my own company, which would eventually become one of the largest and most reputable online hypnosis download websites in the world. I was given an ultimatum that would forever change not only the course of my own future, but the lives of many others I've encountered in the past 21 years.

My boss, where I worked as a stockbroker, received a copy of the business license paperwork one day and called me into his office. He told me I had 30 days to decide between my current job, where I made a very comfortable living, and my new business where more money was going out than coming in.

I was faced with the startling statistics that 8 out of 10 businesses fail and even more daunting, over 90% of online businesses fail within the first 120 days. Beyond that, 95% of all new products also fail. Backed by all those lovely statistics, coupled with the fact that:

- I did not have a background in running a business.
- I did not have a college degree.
- I did not even have a business plan.
- I was not yet ready to make my sole living as an entrepreneur.
- I was going to leave behind two years of company stock I had put 25% of my income into.
- I was single and had no other means of supporting myself.

I had a choice to make.

I'm sure you can take a wild guess at what I decided.

What business strategy did I have?

It was the same strategy I used when I was around 5 years old and I met an extremely obese woman, whom I was related to and I made the decision that I was never going to end up that way. At 51 years old, I currently weigh 130 pounds and I've never weighed over 168. Yet everyone else in my family has hit at least 250. Some as much as 600 pounds.

It's the same strategy I used when I was in first

grade and saw the 6th graders were putting on the play - The Wizard of Oz - and I made up my mind in that very moment that when I was in 6th grade, I would play Dorothy (and I did).

It's the same strategy you're using right now as you choose to use the power of the words in this book to create a transformation in your mindset from one of powerless, to one of power, to change any area of your life.

It's a strategy you've been using unknowingly your whole life. It's the energy that has worked through you and given you that extra push to get through the most difficult and challenging moments of your life.

It's called Hope.

It this book, my cherished friend and respected colleague Richard Nongard, along with his esteemed co-author, Randy Dobbs, you will discover the power of hope.

As an author of a book based on the concept of Law of Attraction, I must admit that prior to delving into this book, I had an issue with the word, 'hope'. It was not surprising however to realize these two highly successful, specialists in the world of leadership and transformation, were not talking about the airy-fairy, cross-your-fingers, maybe, we'll see what happens, wishful or tentative thinking, context of this word.

No, what they are discussing in this book is about the very substance that breathes life into your desires, stimulates creative thinking, and encourages us to believe in what is possible.

Hope, as a strategy, will cause you to take action on what is most important to you. It's a state of mind that drives positive, inspired emotion. It's about transcending fears, which all too often block people from even being able to admit to a desire they have or envision a brighter future for themselves.

It's the very essence which allows one to tap into their unrealized genius, the lack of which is where your desires come to die.

Real Hope: How Hope Drives Positive Actions That Lead to Business, Leadership, and Real-World Victory offers readers true stories and practical strategies anyone can use to tap into that place which has the ability to be the game-changer and a turning point in their life.

Even a one-time read could be the very thing that causes one to transcend a life of normalcy to a life that is extraordinary and beyond your wildest desires.

From a leadership standpoint, you'll learn how hope is the foundation of transformation. In order to be a leader, you need to have or develop the trait of inspiring others. People will not do what you want them to do for very long unless they feel inspired. To be a leader of others, one must first be a leader of oneself. To be inspiring to others, one must first be inspired. How can there be inspiration without hope? There isn't.

Throughout the pages of this book, Real Hope gently persuades a question to arise from within, "How can I be a source of hope for my fellow human?" The answers to this question are articulately and thoughtfully woven in as you take a journey through real, heartfelt stories and apply the guidance of the practical ideas and timely strategies.

Having discussed leadership at great length many times with Richard, I personally know his deep understanding in transformational leadership

The collaboration with Randy Dobbs, who has mentored dozens of top executives at fortune 500 CEOs for decades, multiplies the realness and dominion that real hope absolutely leads to real success.

Their stories alone, of incredible triumphs when most would have given up hope, make this book a no-brainer for anyone to add to their list of "Must-reads", whether or not you (yet) identify yourself as a leader.

This book has given hope a new meaning to me. My hope is that you will allow the words you're about to read inspire you to make the choice to be hopeful, and that you use it in your leadership to instill that hope in the lives of others.

Thank you, Richard and Randy, for the honor and privilege of sharing my thoughts with your readers.

Victoria M. Gallagher
Scottsdale, AZ

Victoria, is the #1 Best Selling Author of *Practical Law of Attraction: Align Yourself with the Manifesting Conditions and Successfully Attract Your Desires.*

Preface

MY OPTIMISM AND hope transported me far from my humble roots as a child with an alcoholic and abusive family — to the very top of the American corporate ladder. I have always held hope high, recognizing it to be the one thing that no one could ever take away from me. Hope carried me far away from the tough family situation I grew up in and eventually helped me win in the cutthroat world of corporate America.

However, I never knew how much hope I could develop and how much hope would be required of me until my only daughter (who had given birth only six weeks earlier) was given six to eight months to live after being diagnosed with stage 4 pancreatic cancer. As her doctor delivered her diagnosis, he promised to make our daughter's last six months as comfortable as possible.

There was no hope in his voice. I felt angry; my daughter lost it and looked to me for comfort and reassurance — I, in my shock and pain, felt that I was unequal to the task. At that moment, I almost succumbed to the idea that there was no hope for her other than comfort and palliative care.

However, after only a moment of this, I realized that no matter how hopeless that previous situation had felt, hope had always been a strategy I could rely on. I promised my daughter to hold onto hope and to find a solution; I would seek out the best doctors in the universe. I was frightened; I am not an expert in medicine or in aggressive or experimental cancer treatments. But I am experienced in hope, and this hope provided me with the strength to make a promise that I didn't even know if I could keep: to become the CEO of her medical care and to find a miracle for her, my new grandson and my family.

This book is not a theoretical book. It is not a philosophical book. It is about the power of real hope to change lives in a variety of adverse situations. My co-author and I hope that in your business, in your leadership, and in all other areas of your life, you will discover that hope is a winning strategy. It has been for me. At the time of this writing, my daughter is one of the fortunate 4% with her type of pancreatic cancer to remain alive after more than five years after her diagnosis. Hope is what got us there. It is the only thing we had the day of her diagnosis, and the power of hope to guide us has been a godsend in every other area of our lives.

We wrote this book both as an inspiration and a practical guide. Take our ideas and live them each day in your family, your business, your community, and in the world.

Randy Dobbs
Greenville, SC

Prologue

THIS BOOK IS an inspiring collection of thoughts and stories about hope and how it has extraordinarily affected the lives of so many wonderful people. This book will enlighten you as to how you can apply this unassuming awareness to better your life as well. Although this book may seem short on pages, it is long on the concept of hope.

The stories, thoughts, feelings, and beliefs are shared by Mr. Randy Dobbs and Dr. Richard K. Nongard, the authors of this book. Randy Dobbs is the former CEO of General Electric, Capital IT Solutions and Phillips Medical System North America. Dr. Richard K. Nongard is a world-renowned therapist and businessman. Both are amazing men, successful, published authors and professional speakers on the concept of hope and transformation.

Within these pages, Randy opens up and shares his experiences about his daughter, who, at age 30, was diagnosed with pancreatic cancer. In 2015, he gave a very emotional TEDx presentation in Charleston, South Carolina entitled, "The Business of Hope." The subject of his TEDx Talk was his daughter, who at the time was 35 years old and had just reached the five-year mark in her battle against stage 4 pancreatic cancer. Yes, you read that correctly. At the time of this writing, eight years later, she continues to battle stage 4 pancreatic cancer. This journey has been the result of many things: key treatments, surgeries, amazing doctors, and people too numerous to mention, who have all contributed to this amazing fight. However, the one thing that binds together every minute element of this amazing story is the power of HOPE!

Dr. Nongard is an amazing author, speaker, therapist, and businessman. After spending many years serving as a mental health professional to some of the toughest, most difficult cases, he became one of the leading authorities in his field. However, in 2014, after waking up unable to speak, he was diagnosed with a potentially life-threatening growth in his throat at the base of his tongue. For the better part of two years, he had no voice, and thus, he lacked the basic tool of his trade. In this book, Richard shares the thoughts and emotions he experienced throughout this amazing journey. He also shares the core ideas from his TEDx Oklahoma City talk entitled, "Why Not Transform?" From his experiences, you will learn about the powerful concept of hope, the hope that comes from learning to master the present moment, and some real-world solutions for making lasting transformations in your life!

To view these TEDx talks, visit
www.RealHopeBook.com

Hope is the key success factor in both of these incredible life stories. Within the subsequent pages of this book, they will address this powerful thing called hope. Richard and Randy are both true believers in the power of hope — and not just in the battle against cancer or the complete loss of one's voice. They have both experienced, refined, and now inspire, assure and teach the power of hope in business and how it transforms companies, leaders, and their communities. They have seen and experienced, firsthand, the power of hope and how it changes lives, mends relationships, and creates the type of life many people desire to have. They have seen it strengthen the faith of others, as well as their own.

Hope is what is most needed across many tough fronts in the world today. This can and will be possible if our religious, government, and business leaders, as well as families and individuals from all walks of life, truly embrace "Real Hope!" As you will find within the pages of this book, hope is about living in the present and taking immediate action. Enjoy your journey.

Part I

What Is Hope?

WHAT DO A Special Forces team pinned down by crossfire in a foreign land, Thomas Edison (with his multiple incandescent lamp failures), a young pitcher going to the mound with a potential no-hitter in the bottom of the ninth, and a new young female mayor going in front of her city council for her first time, all have in common? The answer is of course: HOPE! Despite their preparations or their predicaments, they all have or had hope for their desired outcome.

Hope can be described in numerous ways. It can be used as both a noun and a verb. Hope can be defined as the feeling of <u>wanting</u> something to happen and <u>thinking</u> that it <u>is possible</u>. Hope can also be defined as <u>someone</u> or <u>something</u> that may be able to provide help. Someone or something is, in other words, that which gives us reason to believe it could happen.

As for this book and our definition of hope, for starters, we view hope as a state of mind that drives positive emotions, energizes, and provides direction. Hope is more than simply a state of mind or a feeling — it is the basis for action.

The concept of hope dates all the way back to ancient writings from the twelfth century and has been recognized throughout time as an offering of faith for the hopeless. Hope is and has been the common thread amongst popular religions around the world and throughout time. The prophet Jeremiah declared, "Our hope is in you", eluding to trust as the mechanism of hope. Throughout much of the Old Testament, hope helped individuals through their tough times as they hoped to be delivered from their enemies. It helped the sick, who were hoping to recover from numerous illnesses and issues. In the New Testament, however, hope moves from trust to action. Paul writes about placing hope in God, and Paul announces that Jesus Christ is our hope. In the Christian faith tradition, hope comes as a gift from God through grace. Hope leads to joy. In total, hope is written in the Bible 129 times.

"Hope is not a strategy", is a cliché proclaimed,

time after time, in business, in economics, schools, and communities, but we want to challenge that statement. Hope <u>is</u> a strategy and, in some situations, the only strategy available — often relegated to the last strategy. Think of the classic science fiction films where the world is facing impending doom and imminent destruction. It is at this point in the film when our hero responds to the question of "Now what?" with the cool proclamation, "Now we hope." Politicians have pounded the idea of "Keep hope alive" into us, and Bill Clinton even campaigned on hope as the "boy from Hope" — a reference both to the name of the city where he was born and to how he overcame his broken family.

Hope is something we believe in. More than a feeling, hope is a strategy; it is a foundation for positive action. Hope propels people to take action in business, leadership, and in every aspect of real life.

Napoleon Bonaparte stated, "A leader is a dealer in hope." He understood it as a strategy to move people.

Hellen Keller understood that hope is the foundation for accomplishment. She said,

"Optimism is the faith that leads to achievement. Nothing can be done without hope and confidence."

Deborah Mills wrote one of the most profound thoughts on hope in her Harvard Business Review blog: "Hope is a critical part of achieving a strategy when based on what is possible; perhaps not highly probable, but possible. Hope is the belief that something is possible and probable and the recognition that the degree of each is not necessarily equal. When hope is based on real-world experience, knowledge, and tangible and intangible data, it results in trust, which is necessary to implement any strategy."

Elon Musk has largely mastered the idea of hope articulated by Mills. He understands how things are possible even when they are not probable. It is for this reason that, despite the difficulties at Tesla Motors in everything from production to corporate structure (highly publicized by the press), Elon Musk is producing the first mass-market electric car and changing the automotive industry forever. His hope that this possibility existed led him to create the Boring Company, which now has contracts to dig super hyperloops as the answer to worldwide traffic congestion. Also, his SpaceX Company has already executed many successful rocket tests with the hope of exploring space in a way that even NASA has not yet been able to do.

Hope is a mindset; it is a strategy and a foundation for action. Most importantly, however, hope is something YOU can believe in.

Hope Is Now

WHEN RICHARD PRESENTED his TEDx talk in Oklahoma City, he quoted the Great Master, Oogway (the turtle and Kung Fu Master from the Kung Fu Panda movies), stating: "Yesterday is history, tomorrow is a mystery; all we have is the present, and that is why it is a gift."

How many times have you heard people say things like, "This is hopeless"? We believe that when someone says and/or feels this way, they are taking the easy way out or failing to act. Hope is not a miracle, but an action associated with the "now" — an action that could very well help facilitate outcomes that approach miracle status.

Far too many times, we find ourselves unsure of our ability to drive change, and often, those changes could lead to positive outcomes in real life. The key to facilitating those possibilities is acting on our hope by using it to trigger action in the now. So, instead of just saying, "I hope that (fill in the blank)", hope must be a commitment to act now in an effort to make the uncertain more certain, the unperceivable perceivable, and the undoable doable! History teaches us that the real heroes throughout time are not those who simply hoped, but those who took immediate actions driven by those hopes!

I am sure that one can remember being told things as a child, like; "You need to clean your room right <u>now</u>" or "<u>Now,</u> you are in trouble." I am sure that each of you, like me, knew that when these types of statements were made, they were a *call to action* or the definition of a situation at that very real time. The statement or use of the word "now" was made to draw attention to a point! So, the point we'd like to draw your attention to is that <u>hope</u>, be it in your relationship, business, personal goals, and virtually any other life activity, is a call to action now!

In essayist Rebecca Solnit's elegy to activism, "Hope in the Dark", she states, "Hope is not a lottery ticket you can sit on the sofa and clutch, feeling lucky. It is an axe you break down doors with, in an emergency." Her rumination, recalling past struggles and how they were overcome, is an act of hope in and of itself.

When Randy Dobbs' daughter, Elizabeth O'Conner, was diagnosed with stage 4 pancreatic cancer at 31 years old and was only given months to live, Randy took his burning desire and relentless hope to not lose his only daughter and began what has now become a nine-year journey. His hope, drive and faith have been breaking down doors to facilitate her survival, following major surgeries, clinical trials, and people on her care team — too numerous to mention — and instilling hope to make her a fighter as well! At the time of this writing, their relentless hope is keeping her alive.

It is important to understand that our adage, "hope is now" is not a metaphor, but an actual element of truth and a call to action. The fact is, the only time that actually exists is right now. This is fundamental in understanding how to act on hope. By staying in the present, you activate the power of now, the power of this very moment, to take action. And for some, the way to turn hopelessness into hope might be as simple as taking a breath.

Mindfulness is the habit of staying in the moment, but more importantly, it is a way of hoping! Have you ever wondered, "How do I hope?" What is the action of hoping? It is, in some ways, being grounded in the present and mindfully knowing that all is not hopeless.

When we remain fully present in the moment, no matter how depressing, overwhelming, or anxiety-producing our thoughts and feeling are, it can bring hope. Psalm 46:10 is a scripture that is so comforting to people that it is almost universally known: "Be still and know that I am God." When we bring our attention to this moment, and only this moment, you can almost feel hope build.

We transform hopelessness into hope by living fully in the moment. Hope is not something for the future; it is for right now. Take in a breath right now. Pay attention to the pages of this book and focus on your breath. Let everything not present in this moment stay outside this moment, and just breathe. Cultivating mindfulness is not difficult, but it takes practice. Paying attention to this moment allows us to fully harness the power of action that our hope gives us.

Hope Transforms
Misery & Fear

THERE IS CLEARLY an unstoppable power in the power of hope. Where better to use/ apply that influence than to power through one's misery or fears. No matter how bad things may look in any area of our lives, those that don't just survive but thrive are those who see hope as this book describes it. They see hope as determination, a unique level of confidence, and a gift; a gift we have all been blessed with. Hope is why you must never give up. Steady efforts full of hope absolutely transform fear or misery into just another life obstacle to overcome.

In the business world, a.k.a. the real world, there are countless stories of how hope produced success. One of the most enthralling stories of hope and faith in our modern history is the story of the 65-year-old man living on $99 per month (social security). Determined to better the last years of his life, he set out to sell his only prized possession, his secret recipe for fried chicken. After being told "no" one thousand and nine times, he was finally told "yes." That was in 1962. To this day, Kentucky Fried Chicken, KFC, is still the biggest and most popular chicken restaurant chain in the world. Other stories of ignoring the "no's" and searching for the "yes's" include Oprah Winfrey, who was told that she lacked the talent and looks to ever have a career in broadcasting. Walt Disney was even fired from his job as a newspaper writer because he had no imagination. J.K. Rowling and Steven King were both rejected over and over and over before they finally heard "yes." Today, the Harry Potter franchise is worth over fifteen billion dollars. Mr. King's empire is worth even more. Even Bill Gates failed many times before the success of Microsoft. And then there is the Ford Motor Company. This is actually Henry Ford's third, yes third motor company! What happened to the first one? The first company went bankrupt before they ever even produced a single car. His second attempt, which actually had a name, The Detroit Car Company, also went bankrupt. In business, we view failure as the opportunity to apply our faith, hope, and experiences toward success.

Randy, like Richard, has found himself in numerous life situations that could be viewed as hopeless and miserable. The list is long, and we will forego the details, but here is a list of the more notable events that either one or both of them had faced, including: abusive step-fathers, alcoholic parents, dysfunctional mothers, major job demotions/losses, divorce(s), multiple business relocations, and financial insecurities. In all these issues, they never believed or, more eloquently put, they never decided that on any occasion or challenge were their lives hopeless.

Where there is hope, there is life and a way forward. Hope has never disappeared, because one can refuse to accept any of this misery as hopeless. As one reflects on that, it could be frightening to some, as they ponder where their life could have ended up if not for the belief that hope is invincible, even in times of greatest misery. Hope gives us something important in transforming and overcoming misery. The heart of hope is psychological flexibility. It is because of hope that we know misery won't last forever, or that fear is the new normal. Hope is what provides flexibility in difficult times, and the value of psychological flexibility is immeasurable.

Psychologists who study misery, anxiety, fear, depression, and any other myriad of negative emotions almost always come to the same conclusion: Psychological flexibility is key. This is the heart of resilience, a concept so important that the U.S. military has spent millions of dollars researching ways to help soldiers develop psychological flexibility and manifest resilience. It has proven to be a solution to some of the problems associated with PTSD, and in some cases, a way of preventing the development of post-traumatic stress entirely (in situations where its development was the norm).

How is psychological flexibility developed? By making hope a verb and by using hope as a strategy. It pulls us out of our depressions, stops our fears in its tracks, and makes a miserable situation a little bit better by refocusing one's attention on the desired result and the probability of achieving it. This does not mean that every aspect of life will be peaches and cream, but it does mean that by activating hope as a bridge from misery to acceptance, or from fear to confidence, that we have avoided making things worse.

When we stop making things worse, there is only one way for things to go; they start to improve. For some, the transformation is rapid and profound; for others, slower and less intense. However, this reality will always materialize for those who use hope as a strategy.

So, what is it you fear? How long have you been dealing with a miserable situation? Have you had hope that it would change? If so, was it the hope mentioned by Rebecca Solnit as a "clutched lottery ticket"? We believe in the unstoppable power of hope, but you must act! To resolve your fear or miseries and in order to transform these issues, hope <u>must</u> become a verb in your life.

Hope Transforms Lives

I<small>N THIS INCREDIBLY</small> powerful chapter, we <u>hope</u> to prove that hope not only has the power to change lives, but that hope is what transforms lives. As we discussed earlier, hope is a word that most of us use every day. Did you catch our use of it in the second sentence above? As you reflect on the day that just passed, how many times did you hope?

When Randy was asked about this list of <u>hopes</u> today, his response was: "This morning, I <u>hoped</u> that the appliance repairman would arrive before noon. I <u>hoped</u> my new doctor would find a better explanation for my back pain. I <u>hoped</u> the lease on our vacant commercial building would be signed by the end of the week. I hoped to get the laundry before closing. I <u>hoped</u> I would be able to speak with my daughter about her cancer treatment before bedtime. There are likely more times that "I hoped" today, but those examples are sufficient to make my point." Some of these events are certainly more significant than others. However, in each event, hoping led to thoughts and actions that transformed his life daily.

We can hope for something simple, like the chance to do the laundry today or to get the car washed tomorrow, for example. However, it can also be critical or complex; we can hope to survive the financial implications of having a large commercial space that might not produce enough revenue next month or we can hope that our daughter will continue to survive her life-threatening disease. Hope, to Randy, is a reminder to continue to act with a <u>confident expectation</u> that a positive outcome will be achieved on all these fronts. Hope is what strengthens his faith that through belief, action, and dealing with reality, he can transform his life every day!

In most instances, hope focuses on the future, but the action driven by hope places us into the now. When we believe, via hope, that we can have a positive and desirable life transformation, we truly start to look at the possibilities that surround us very differently.

Randy loves sports and truly loves to see the

underdog pull off the upset. This past year, he got to see a local high school football team upset a much better team in the season-ending playoffs. What was most surprising about this upset was that the better team had defeated the underdog (by a score of 48 to 7) during the regular season — a true butt-whipping! After the game, he talked to the coach of the victorious underdog and asked him "How did you transform the performance (lives) of your players going into a game you supposedly had no chance to win?" He said there are four key things that occur in such an upset.

1. The coach instills hope. He ensures the players have hope that they can achieve an upset.

2. The coach facilitates the reality of that hope by setting up small wins during the course of the game, like being tied at the end of the first quarter or only being down by seven points at halftime.

3. The coach sets up a detailed game plan to achieve small wins along the way

4. Achieving small wins via the game plan <u>turns the players' hope into belief that they can win.</u> When they <u>believe</u> in themselves

and their ability to win the game, the team becomes very dangerous as an underdog. That is the power of hope!

Hope does transform lives through belief and action. If this was untrue, polio would, more than likely, still threaten our lives; no underprivileged would ever attend college, Kennedy's quest to reach the moon would have failed, and many of us would live in a much different world than we do now. Hope is transformative!

One of the most powerful ways to understand how hope transforms lives is to look at the ways hope has already transformed your own life. Think back to a time when something wonderful happened in your own life, such as a graduation, a new relationship, a career goal that was accomplished. Even if recent memory has been clouded by difficulty, and you have to go back a long time, there has probably been some point in life where you hoped fervently, and the outcome was amazing.

Richard reflects on selling greeting cards door to door back when he was about eight years old. He hoped he could sell enough cards to make money for a camping tent. And he did! He remembers, with a smile on his face, going door to door in the cold Chicago winter, explaining that, in the summer, he would be going to Boy Scout camp and needed a tent. The people that he showed the cards to responded. It was his very first success as a businessman. An effective strategy often used whenever one is struggling in the present with business is to think back to the innocent hope we once embraced and believed with all our hearts. Faith and hope are what led that eight-year-old boy to knock on each door. Are you ready to start knocking? Let's go!

Hope Is Real!

A<small>T THIS POINT</small>, I believe the previous chapters bear witness to just how real that we believe hope is every day. Fundamentally, we believe that the energy with which we power through each day's issues and opportunities is fueled by hope. It is tough, but the reality is that steady effort must be applied to accomplish anything; that reality of steady effort is fueled by hope. On the other hand, we achieve hope from our steady effort to face and deal with reality. Hope drives hope! What is more real than the power and discipline associated with hope?

As mentioned earlier in the book, there is likely no place where hope is more referred to than in <u>the Bible</u>. Many verses talk about how real hope is by referencing hope in God. Biblical hope not only looks towards the future for something good, but it also has a clear expectation that it will happen. (Jeremiah 29:11): "For I know the plans I have for you, plans to prosper you and not harm you, plans to give you hope and a future." (Romans 15:13): "May the God of hope fill you with all joy and peace as you trust in him, so that you may overflow with hope by the power of the Holy Spirit." (Romans 8:24): "For in this hope, we were saved. But hope that is seen is no hope at all. Who hopes for what they already have?" (Romans 8:25): "But if we hope for what we do not yet have, we wait for it patiently." I believe that these verses clearly support that hope, in this case hope in God, is providing <u>real</u> confidence and direction looking forward.

Now that we have thought about hope being real, let's talk about real hope and its power. Hope is never more real to many of us than when hope is at the center of a solution to an issue that is bigger than we are. There are many examples of this, but it is impossible to speak about real hope without speaking about my daughter. When the first oncologist told my daughter that she had pancreatic cancer, she quickly followed with how sorry she was and how she would work to provide her with the best quality of life in the months she had left to live. That was now over nine years ago, and my daughter is still with us, which is a true miracle, given her particular cancer. From that day in 2010 until today, I have hoped for my daughter to beat this disease, and I have worked hard to instill that same hope in her so that she can beat cancer. That is the power of hope. Real hope has fueled my continuous actions to find doctors and treatments. Those actions have fueled her real hope to live. Her fighting this most deadly cancer and winning has fueled the hope of similar patients. The hopes of many patients have fueled the amazing effort of many doctors and other professionals to continue to study this disease and create more tools/medicines to improve survival rates. All of this is fueling the fundraising and focus of many around the globe to defeat pancreatic cancer in the near future. That is how real the power of hope is and will always be. One person, one family, and one doctor with real hope can change the future!

We clearly believe that there is significant power in real hope. We do not believe this because of biblical scripture or some other books/articles that we read. We believe this because without the benefit and power of hope in our lives, we would be less effective husbands, fathers, employees, leaders, or friends. This is not magic or some big secret. This is about accepting and acting on your hopes. Hope, real hope, is life's greatest treasure, available to all!

Hope is real! It's interesting that so many people question whether hope is real, but they never seem to question if hopelessness is real. We know hope is real because history is filled with examples of how hope saved the day. Christopher Reeves played Superman in the iconic 1980s movie based on the best-selling comic books. Reeves was catapulted to the highest levels of Hollywood fame and success. Then, in a tragic horseback riding accident, he became a quadriplegic.

Reeves' hope was all he had left, and it was hope that made him a real-life superman. His hope for a medical breakthrough compelled him to use his talents and resources in a way that might help future spinal-cord injury survivors live better lives. He gave hope to others; he did not only inspire awareness in the non-profit medical research space, but his foundation gave techno-logically-advanced wheelchairs to other paralysis victims to give them hope of living a more typical life and doing things that they previously had been unable to do.

Reeves famously said, "When we have hope, we discover powers within ourselves we may have never known: the power to make sacrifices, to endure, to heal, and to love. Once we choose hope, everything is possible."

Reeves knew hope was real, and he knew the value of hope. He also knew that hope was a choice, and that choice was a daily decision between hope and hopelessness. By choosing to hope, we make hope a reality in our lives and bring it into the present moment.

Tyler George had hope. He had hope that the rainforest could be preserved, that the indigenous people of the Ecuadorian rainforest could create self-sustaining communities, and that he could build a business around bringing hope to others. George was one of the first "social entrepreneurs" to prove that a sustainable business could be built on hope. His brand, RUNA, has thrived in the competitive energy beverage space for more than a decade. It is hope that has been the mechanism for land management, sustainable farming, and direct trade relationships with local producers. It is the reality of hope that has made this all possible.

When have you seen hope in your own life? When have you known hope was real?

At that time, when I, Richard Nongard, lost my voice completely, I still had hope. Yes, it was hard to see it at times, and I certainly did not feel it always, but I knew that hope was present. For me, hope has always been like a building foundation. There may be a lot going on up above, but in the end, even if the storms blow everything else way, the foundation remains.

At that time, a few years ago, I moved my home, and I moved my business 2000 miles away. I was not even sure what my goal was, but everything had been blown down. I had been defeated by significant health problems and significant problems in just about every area of life. What is ironic is that I moved to one of the cities known for hope — Las Vegas. Hopeful gamblers have been coming here for decades, but gold miners and silver panners have been hoping in this area for over a century.

Las Vegas is where entertainers come hoping for their big break and where businesses have come in hopes of a new future. Companies like Amazon, Tesla and Panasonic have all come to

Nevada to seek their fortunes, just as the gold miners did 150 years ago. That is why I came here. I was at a point in life where I did not have a plan; I only had that foundation of hope.

The result? Because hope is real, I was able to build on it. My business model changed, my personal life thrived, and what I have today is stronger than anything I have ever had in life. Hope is real. It is the foundation that is often unseen, but in reality, is holding everything else up.

— Story One —

Real Life Application in Business

W HEN WE INTRODUCED this book, we talked extensively about what hope is. A simple summary of what we said is that hope is both action and faith. The following story is a perfect example of how instilling faith and following through with action can and does change lives.

A quick back note about our authors before we start the story: *They say 7% of Americans have a drinking problem, and half of them are alcoholics. Randy and Richard both know the pain of this statistic firsthand. Both experienced lost childhoods, emotional traumas, and the devastation of growing up in alcoholic homes. They both hoped for something unknown to them; after all, a kid growing up in a dysfunctional home doesn't really know anything different. They did, however, both know they didn't want it to be the same when they became adults.*

And now, on with the story. Drug screening is a common part of modern hiring practices. Businesses also conduct random drug tests on their current employees, fire employees with addiction problems, and avoid the liability of dealing with alcoholic and substance-abusing employees. No doubt our parents at one time or another brought added burdens to our families by being on the firing line of these ideas.

One company that Randy recently became acquainted with (we'll call them XYZ Company) does things in the completely opposite way. This company actively seeks out and hires convicts, those who have struggled to maintain sobriety, and people whom that almost any other business would never hire or would terminate upon discovery of their backgrounds. Company XYZ is a consumer appliance retail operation with multiple stores and provides sales and customer service, both onsite and in their customers' homes. For a business to even consider taking on the liability of placing ex-cons, alcoholics, and drug addicts in their customers' homes, they clearly are operating from a strategy of hope and faith. Randy learned about this company's philosophies when his washer and dryer were delivered. The two young delivery men from XYZ company could not have been more polite, hardworking, and happy to be doing their job on a Saturday. In fact, they were so good that it prompted him to engage them to discuss their employer and job satisfaction. Each of them said their employer was great, and <u>they</u> had never had a better work situation. That prompted him to ask how long they had worked there and what made it so special. Their answer stopped him dead in his tracks! They had both been employed less than a year, and they had left a half-way house and incarceration prior to their current jobs. From there, they talked at length about how they felt and what this chance meant to them.

It was then that Randy saw the real power of hope at work. They, in the months before, had no hope. Which meant they had no plans for a better life and no joy. This company's program, which is grounded in the hope of changing these young men's lives, has instilled a hope in them that is broad and includes a future with lots of plans. Nothing we have witnessed better paints the picture of how hope, and actions based on that hope, transform misery and fear!

We believe that to not only believe in but to seek out people with real issues that have no hope is hope in its finest hour. How could you instill hope in others through your business? Don't get us wrong, we are not advocating that the only way to succeed is to house, employ, or become close to convicts, addicts, and people with the difficulties as those we have described above; however, we are sure there is a child or an elderly adult in your neighborhood that has lost hope for a variety of reasons. Can you take them a meal? Can you give them a job to do around the house? Can you even just tell them, "I am thinking about you". Think about what a world we would have if we all put hope into action, even if we did it differently than this company has done.

The first five chapters of this book focused on five ideas:

- What is hope?
- Hope is now.
- Hope transforms misery and fear.
- Hope transforms life.
- Hope is real.

Many people, such as those struggling with an addiction, need to see hope and the actions associated with it as a better alternative. So many people are blessed to the extent that they never need to worry about their next meal, their next rent payment, or their source of medical support. However, for a growing number of people, the need for hope, and the actions associated with it, is something they need now. Those who face hunger, shelter, and physical issues need to believe that there are answers to their problems, and those answers can only be facilitated by "dealers in hope"! Hope is either focused on the now or it becomes a dream versus a hope. Hope today instills faith in a better tomorrow.

The power of hope to transform lives at Company XYZ has been instilled in the employees hired right out of the halfway house and in their children, significant others, and community. This transformation has not only directly benefitted these stakeholders with stable jobs and monthly income, but the spirit of hope, throughout the management, staff, ownership and even the customers of the business, is apparent just from walking in the door of any of their retail locations.

Have you ever been to a business where morale is low, workers feel dread, not hope, and where the feeling you get is unwelcoming? Of course you have. This describes many of our nation's dying retail sectors. This shop is different, though; the feeling is alive and hopeful. What is the reason? Lives are being transformed. Years ago, the owner of the business was given hope by someone who was willing to take a risk on him. In turn, he has taken a risk on others. He knows something — it is a low risk because hope has the power to transform lives. The rewards for his business have been lower staff turnover, higher customer satisfaction, and great financial success in a low-margin business where many competitors closed their doors years ago.

Hope is real because it is an action. As we stated previously in these pages, hope is not something that is going to happen or that we want to happen in the future. Hope is present in this moment, and all we have to do is activate it. Company XYZ is a hopeful place. The managers, employees, and ownership know that it an effective strategy in a competitive market. When these employees wake up in the morning with purpose and head to work at a place where they feel joy at work and get a paycheck, that paycheck is a paper certificate that may as well be a diploma in hope!

Part II

Hope Is the Cornerstone of Great Leadership

THE METAPHOR OF the cornerstone comes from the idea that the first stone set in a masonry foundation will determine the placement of every other stone in a building and the strength the structure will derive from proper placement. The cornerstone of great leadership is always hope. Strategically, it gives strength to leaders and creates a foundation among stakeholders that follows the lead that hope offers.

Great leaders are hopeful. Great leaders share a message of hope. Great leaders live a life that finds hope in every situation, and great leaders manifest new opportunities because of hope. History is replete with examples of great leaders who had hope. Abraham Lincoln famously said, "My dream is a place and a time where America will once again be seen as the last best hope of earth." In the devastation of the civil war, Lincoln saw hope as the cornerstone that would make or break the future of the country.

As a leader, what attention have you paid to hope? Have you had high hopes for yourself, and instilled hope in others? In my TEDx talk in Oklahoma City, I (Richard) shared my story of coming from a broken home, my father's death from alcoholism at age 42, and a multi-generational set of problems that actually began when my great-great-great-great-grandfather came to America as a trader and became best known for committing the first murder in the new city of Chicago. I share my own experiences being in handcuffs for public intoxication at age twenty-two and being offered a choice by the arresting officer to essentially get help or go to jail. At that moment, I hoped I could break my family's cycle of addiction, and that one day, when I had children, they would grow up with a different experience.

That night changed my life. I got the help that I needed and that my father never sought. I had watched my dad drink Hamm's beer night after night and fall asleep in the living room and never go to work. My now-adult children have never seen me drunk or even take a drink. The last drink I had was on March 31, 1988 — over 31 years ago. My oldest son is 28.

In parenting, I had no plan, I had no example, and like many, I become a parent without much planning other than living in the moment. All I had was hope. For the past 28 years, I have clung to hope as the cornerstone of my family leadership. The result? My three children are amazing. One has a career in the military, is now assigned as an infantry drill sergeant, and earned the combat infantry badge in Iraq. My daughter is a speech-language pathology graduate who works with children, and my youngest son has a master's degree in economics and works as an analyst. My nine-year-old step-daughter is bilingual and comes home from school every day filled with joy. I know that joy stems from the hope I have for our family.

I know that I am fortunate. Some of my friends have been less fortunate in parenting than I have been, and some have suffered severe tragedy and hardships as a result of their children. Hope was how I provided leadership to my family. I hoped for a better life and paid attention to their hopes and dreams. When they had a hard day, I promised them tomorrow would be better, which was a promise I could only make because I had hope.

I am proud of my family; the odds were stacked against us, but hope has reigned over the past three decades, and the result has been amazing.

Leaders make hope the cornerstone of great leadership in their families, in their communities, in their businesses, and in every aspect of life. Hope is the cornerstone of great leadership and opens the door to prosperity. Without hope, we cannot aspire to greatness. Without hope, we will not have the energy to lead. Without hope, we do not find the strategies for navigating the difficulties of life, many of which come to us through providence rather than desire; but hope is always the path leadership takes to find a solution.

Author Simon Bailey shared, in his TEDx talk *Be the Boom! Breaking the Sound Barriers in Education,* that hope is a better predictor of academic success and graduation rates than test scores. In discussing leadership, Bailey has elsewhere pointed out that, "Whether you have a leadership title or not, you have the potential to either lead your organization beyond all expectations or inhibit its growth through entropy." We would suggest that the difference is made by either having hope as the cornerstone of leadership or hopelessness as the cornerstone of missed leadership opportunity.

In the first section of the book, we wrote about hope as a verb or a word that meant actions, such as, "The pitcher 'hoped' he could retire the side in the ninth inning and achieve a no-hitter." It was a clear call to action for one more inning of tough work. This is opposed to hope as an adjective where little good is expected, such as, "It was a hopeless game as the team walked on the field with their star quarterback injured."

So, if hope is a call to action or an expectation of a happening, it has to be the cornerstone of leadership. What leader, with any expectation of success or greatness, would approach his role as a leader without a bias for action and/or success? To maintain hope as a leader in all that you do is to maintain a vision of what you believe can be accomplished. In fact, hope is not a choice in great leadership, but rather, it is a mandate necessary to think and act as any great leader.

I (Randy Dobbs) have a reputation as a leader who can turn around underperforming businesses. They are classified typically as under-performing because they are not achieving their financial objectives. That can be driven by a lack of leadership, process issues, quality problems, or customer issues. Regardless of the issues, most of the employees of companies that I have worked with have hoped that I was going to be the leader to discover and resolve the problems. Why did they hope for my success? Because they hoped to keep their job. They hoped to make their house payment. They hoped to provide for their families. Those who did not have these hopes were clearly a big part of the problem!

So, as the leader in these tough business situa-tions, did I have hopes? You better believe that, as a leader, I had big hopes and lots of them. I hoped that the issues would be readily visible, and I hoped I would be able to build an effective plan for their resolution. I hoped that the employees would trust me, and I hoped they could believe in me and my communication skills. I hoped that I would find the right talent for the tasks at hand, and I hoped that we could build an action plan that would accomplish significant performance turnaround in 18 months.

These hopes, coupled with my actions and those of my team, facilitated great successes, including a turnaround of the year award in the whole of the General Electric Company in 2001.

It is tough to be a leader in today's world. There is a lot of economic turmoil, and the workforce becomes more complex as do the laws governing many aspects of a successful leader. All those things can and do both impact the leader and his/her employees. So it is imperative to have hope as a cornerstone of leadership, as hope is not just an action; hope is a strong emotional bond that a leader can instill with their authenticity, focus on the future, open and continuous communication, and an emphasis on optimism relative to all challenges. With that cornerstone and lots of work, employees develop, over time, a belief that acts to drive hope to success!

Leaders Inspire Hope

EAL LEADERS INSPIRE hope. They inspire with words. They inspire with actions. They inspire by example. They do this both humbly and while grandstanding to draw attention to hope when all else is failing. Martin Luther King said, "We must accept finite disappointment but never lose infinite hope." What King meant is that leaders maintain hope in every situation and inspire others in both good times and bad.

Leaders inspire hope through the four pathways of inspiration:

1. Genuinely caring about others.
2. Communicating positively.
3. Being an enthusiastic cheerleader for hope.
4. Building others up with every opportunity.

Do you care about others? We doubt you would have gotten this far in a book about hope if you did not care about others. It is probably something that comes naturally to you — something either you have chosen to pass on to others because someone gave you the gifts of compassion and empathy or because, as a result of experiencing a lack of compassion and empathy in your life, you know just how much compassion and empathy can help another person. Regardless of whether it comes naturally, empathy and compassion should be cultivated. Leaders inspire hope by cultivating real compassion and empathy for other people.

This is done by paying attention to people, really getting to know them, and thus, understanding them. Parents cultivate compassion and empathy in their children by sincerely asking every day how their children are, and by attending to them both in good times and bad. There is a great misbelief among modern parents that it is not the quantity of time we spend with our children but rather the quality of that time; in the modern era of split families, this misbelief is easy to buy into. The reality is that children want our time.

We cultivate genuine compassion and

empathy in leadership positions by knowing our community and understanding their desires and needs. Both of us have served on volunteer boards for non-profits. It is easy to be on a board, show up at meetings and donate some cash to help the charity. For many board members, this is exactly what they do. However, compassion and empathy are cultivated by meeting with fellow board members and by inquiring of paid staff members in an organization how their work is going and how the board can support them. Empathy and compassion can also be cultivated by knowing and understanding the needs and desires of the constituents served by the organization and by inspiring hope at every opportunity.

Positive communication is an essential strategy for inspiring hope. Studies in both schools and workplace environments show that leaders who stress positive feedback have higher-performing students or employees. Some ways to be a positive communicator include choosing to share kind words and pointing out strengths in others that even they might be unaware they possess. Hope is inspired when leaders communicate positively, and it quells the natural tendency that many have to devalue themselves; it encourages these people to think more optimistically.

Leaders are cheerleaders for inspiring hope. Real leaders encourage others to have hope. Jesse Jackson gave what was one of the most inspiring political speeches of all time in 1988. It was a challenge to hope and dream. He said, "Use hope and imagination as weapons of survival and progress" and ended with a passionate plea to "Keep hope alive", looking the audience and camera in the eye and emphasizing this line four times in a row.

We both have stories of hope that have come from our personal experiences with hardship and success, and we have shared these stories, even when they have been hard to share and exposed our vulnerabilities; we hope to use these stories to inspire hope in others. If you have a story of hope, share it loudly and share it boldly. It is a message that will inspire others and let your hope be the cornerstone of leadership.

Words are powerful. They can start wars, end relationships, and change lives. A sharp word can create a generation of rift and destroy the culture of a company. There are multiple stories of recent company leaders using harsh words "off the record" that have come to public attention. In many of these cases, such words ended the leadership of the speaker, and in other situations, they have even sunk companies' bottom lines. However, words can inspire hope, lead others, and change lives for the better.

Inspiration is defined as "the process of being mentally stimulated to do or to feel something, especially to do something creative." Also, earlier in our writing, we defined hope as a feeling of expectation and desire for a certain thing to happen. When you look at these two definitions, it is simply imperative to me that leaders stimulate some creative action to drive some expectation for change/success. For without true, committed leaders, there would be little inspiration for many of us and the world around us.

As I have shared before, real leaders establish a vision for the future and then share that vision broadly across their respective organizations. That shared vision can encompass many things, but it almost always includes improving the performance and working environment of all involved in the entity.

Well, assuming that just about any leader could create a shared vision, does that make them an inspirational leader? It does not! A truly inspirational leader has the ability to take that shared vision and inspire or stimulate their organization to reach great performance/success through their desire or hope for a number of things, which could include job security, more earnings, job promotions or a better working environment. Most employees do hope for those things and more, but it is amazing how few are actually inspired by leadership with true hope for these accomplishments in the future.

What kind of leader inspires hope and the change/work associated with it across an organization? Leaders that inspire hope will inspire an organization to do their best and contribute because the hope of the shared vision is infectious. That type of leader is a leader who communicates strongly, is driven by a clear set of purposes, and is constantly demonstrating their passion for what is done today, tomorrow and in the future towards that shared vision. People are inspired by a leader who cares for them and their hopes/needs for their successful collective futures.

No leader had a more difficult time inspiring hope, as he led this country through some of the toughest times of change, than Abraham Lincoln. As he struggled with a divided nation, a terrible civil war and political turmoil that pulled at this young nation's very fabric, he often spoke of hope as a leader to inspire a future vision. As a leader who has been tested by some really trying times, I really admire his quote, "I hope to stand firm enough not to go backward, and yet not go forward fast enough to wreck the country's cause." Leaders who inspire hope are constantly trying to balance the reality of today versus the version of tomorrow with authentic/passionate leadership.

Hope Bridges Leadership
From One Generation
to the Next

A LEADERSHIP THAT DIES with a leader isn't really leadership — it is charisma. True leadership creates a transference of power, creativity, action, and vision and penetrates deep among a team and a culture. In other words, it spans the generations, leaving behind a cadre of leaders. In the book *Transformational Leadership: A Blueprint for Real Organizational Change*, Randy Dobbs writes, "A transformational leader's final, most lasting mark is that the transformation doesn't stop when he or she leaves the business." This is the great hope of Transformational Leadership that transcends any other form of leadership.

Steve Jobs was certainly a larger than life figure, as is Bill Gates, and even Howard Shultz, the former CEO of Starbucks. All three of them built a business from the ground up, and all three of them eventually left the business they created. All three of those businesses have continued to flourish even in the absence of larger-than-life leaders. How did that happen? It happened with hope. It happened with intention, and it happened because each one of these leaders knew that what they started was not finished and that it would be up to the next generation to carry out the legacy they created. This was the hope each of these leaders shared.

When I wrote the book *Viral Leadership: Seize the Power of Now to Create Lasting Transformation in Business,* I pointed out that business is like art and literature. It can sustain not just for generations, but even millennia. The same is true in leading a family. Certainly, royal families can be a testament to the longevity of leadership in a family. Think of your own community; which leader in your community still has a legacy that is impacting future generations today?

In Oklahoma, the legacy of Will Rogers reigns throughout the state. Schools are named after him, highways are named after him, and even a county is named after him. His big contribution, though, was not just fame or charisma but a recognition of the future generation. He brought hope to the dustbowl, the Great Depression, and the lives of everyone he spoke to. He was a comedian and commentator, a writer and an actor. He was charismatic. His commitment, though, to not only his home state but the lives of others, and his hope to see a brighter future for the next generation, has created a cadre of leaders across the globe.

How does one use hope as a tool to cross the generational divide? First, by never giving up. Every generation has complained about the successive generations. It is easy to see what is wrong with people who have different opportunities and experiences. However, hope sustains investment in the lives of others. Secondly, hope believes that there is something yet to come, and that is powerful. Hope recognizes that what I have created is incredible but believes in a vision that is yet to be discovered. Lastly, hope builds up a future cadre of leaders because it infuses them with both the tools for success and the will to succeed.

I believe, as we have mentioned repeatedly

in the previous chapters, that hope is a critical foundation of leadership. I believe that if you have continued to read this book that you buy into that belief. With that said, let's reach a little deeper into our thought process and think about hope bridging that leadership across generations. Now don't get me wrong — I don't think hope alone does this. It is hope combined with creativity and relentless effort that bridges leadership from one generation to the next.

A standalone book could be written about famous figures who combined hope and action to bridge leadership across multiple generations. How about George Washington? He led American forces during our war of independence as a young nation. Then, as a leader and, ultimately, the first president of this new country, he instilled hope in the leadership for years to come that this democracy was worth protecting for our future. In fact, I think one of his greatest quotes on hope and future leadership is, "I hope I shall possess firmness and virtue enough to maintain what I consider the most enviable of all titles, the character of an honest man."

Another leader who bridges generations

with hope and leadership was one whom I most admire, Abraham Lincoln. As you know, he was our president during what I consider to be one of our country's most difficult times: The Civil War. He led the union to maintain the United States, and he widened the difficulty of it all by including his efforts to abolish slavery in the United States. We have already mentioned several of his quotes about hope, but I think the most powerful one that bridges leadership across generations is as follows: "Any people anywhere, being inclined and having the power, have the right to rise up and shake off the existing government, and form a new one that suits them better. This is a most valuable — a most sacred right: a right which we hope and believe is to liberate the world." What an amazing message to future generations as he fought to save his current generation!

Now I would like to close with a more common example of hope bridging leadership across generations. I am currently working with a 40-year old, family-owned business as they transition to the next generation of leaders — which will not be family, by the way! The three siblings, who currently lead the business, joined their father 30 years ago; their father took a "hands-on" approach to that leadership bridge. Today, with no family to pass the business to, they have decided to sell the business. Initially, they were not too receptive to new owners with new ways of doing things. However, they have come to realize that their hopes and their legacy are more important than their control. That is the point! Real leadership has true hope for the generational success of a business long after they are gone. So, as stated already so many times in previous chapters, hope is the verb that causes leaders to apply positive action to bridge leadership across generations to ensure the future success of a business. Hope and the power of hope are bigger than any one person or generation.

Hope Invites Future Leadership

TRUE LEADERSHIP SPAWNS forthcoming leaders. Leadership that does not create future leaders is not true leadership; it is most often charisma or a good succession plan. This may lead to short-term financial success in business, but ultimately the true measure of leadership is that it is self-sustaining and invites, encourages, and shapes future leadership. Hope is the invitation to future leadership. Hope invites future leadership by asking for trust and engagement and believing in something permanent. Patek Philippe, a renowned Swiss watch manufacturer, created an iconic advertisement 20 years ago with the line, "You never actually own a Patek Philippe. You merely look after it for the next generation."

In much the same way, leadership is the same.

Leadership is something we have been entrusted with and that we look after until the successive leader is ready.

Effective planning for any future relies on hope. Hope is the common thread that must continuously run through any and every project, event, idea, decision, dream, wish or desire. It matters not what you call it, but it is hope that keeps it alive. We have all seen a family that was held together by a revered patriarch or matriarch but then crumbled upon their death. The adage, "The first generation builds wealth, the second maintains wealth, and the third spends wealth," is a testament to many families not using hope to sustain leadership within a family. Then there are families who have used hope to invite future leadership. A great example is Philanthropist Eunice Kennedy Shiver, who in 1968 created the Special Olympics. She was the daughter of Joseph P. Kennedy, who himself came from a long line of business and political leaders. Her children include TV journalist Maria Shriver and philanthropist Anthony Kennedy Shriver. Anthony serves as the chairman of Best Buddies International (a non-profit organization) and assists millions of people with intellectual and developmental disabilities around the world. He has been leading this charge for 30 years. Anthony says, "If we instill a sense of acceptance in all young people, imagine what a different community we would all share, not to mention how high we would lift our lives and the lives of our 'buddies'." It was his mother's role model of leadership that molded him into the leader he is today, and it was hope that invited him to believe the concept of friendship could impact the lives of millions of people. These are people that had previously lived in the shadows of society, and the Best Buddies program helps them move into a place of dignity, work, and self-efficacy.

There is an immense contrast between the family that falls apart once the matriarch or patriarch is gone and the family that invites, inspires, and nurtures its next generation with hope. These families of hope not only create more wealth but serve others with that wealth. This same philosophy holds true in business. When a successful business leader passes succession to a future leader, that business becomes even more successful. One of the most enthralling and ongoing sagas in the modern business world is the inception and continued success of the Apple

Corporation. Business history will write the final chapter of the Steve Jobs and Tim Cook story, but those who feared that leadership would die without Steve Jobs are now appreciating how Tim Cook has become an even more effective leader in many ways.

Hope invites future leadership in four ways:

- Hope invites future leadership by giving future leaders something to believe in.
- Hope invites future leadership by asking for engagement.
- Hope invites future leadership by creating a culture of leadership.
- Hope invites future leadership by shining the light on what is possible rather than what is impossible.

One of the greatest powers of hope is that it encourages engagement. Companies spend billions of dollars every year attempting to re-engage employees that have become complacent, uninterested and disengaged in their work and with the company they represent. Think back to the first week of your last job. You were filled with hope! It is that hope that engages you, that engages families, communities, and workplaces. They all need to recognize that hope asks for engagement because hope is the light shining the way to a brighter future.

Whether you realize it or not, the culture of leadership impacts every person in an organization, from the person with the title to the person who just came on board. From the CEO pushing the platinum corporate card across to the waiter to the janitor pushing the mop around the bathroom floor, hope invites equal power, opportunity, and inspiration for anyone and everyone. In fact, one of the most successful products ever produced by the Frito-Lay company, and one of the most endearing stories of hope and engagement, is that of the Flaming Hot Cheetos, which was conceived and developed by the Frito-Lays janitor! He is now, by the way, Senior VP of the Latin Marketing Department. Real organizational strength, be it a family, a business, a non-profit, or a movement recognizes that hope creates a culture of leadership by motivating the creation of core values and ensuring that they are communicated from top to bottom.

Hope shines light where there is fear. Hope shines light where there may have previously been failures. Most importantly, hope shines its brightest light on what is possible. The Apostle Paul profoundly pointed out that people don't hope for what they can already see. Hope looks at possibilities, the unlimited possibilities that continue to create and transform generations of leaders.

As we have pointed out throughout the book, hope, in its truest form, is clear emotion, not a skill. It is this hopeful emotion that inspires, motivates, and invites future leadership, which in turn creates hopeful anticipation of what can and will become a better future. Visionary leaders plan for the future and possess the drive to make sure that these plans are executed. Non-visionary leaders are those leaders who experience hope as a wish, and they often wait for someone else to make things happen.

Future visionary leaders have several hopeful traits that drive their leadership success. Hopeful leaders drive change. They do not fear change but, rather, they thrive on change and new opportunities despite the risks associated with them. Hope invites future leadership that is optimistic, as it peers into the future. Randy states in his previous book that leadership for a successful future is about creating a vision for the future that instills hope that, in the days ahead, there will be improved opportunities for individual and organizational success! Hope, as an emotion in leadership, is completely positive and forward-looking. Randy had to paint that picture for an organization of more than 7000 employees in a business losing millions of dollars a year. No one, including him, had the confidence to transform that situation without a strong vision of hope coupled with operational details.

Interestingly, most organizations that need some type of performance improvement are always hopeful and significantly encouraged by leaders who experience hope. Hopeful leaders know that there really is no strong future without a plan. So, it is not emotion alone that invites future leadership; it is the hopeful emotion of a leader <u>with a plan</u> that does what he/she commits to doing. When Randy was at General Electric, he began using what he called "town hall" meetings and weekly emails to the entire organization as a way to communicate his hope, facilitate his vision, report on his commitments and instill hope in the organization that a successful future was not just possible but realistic!

An inspired and hopeful leader is a leader who can see the present issues and needs of a business and imagine and facilitate an improved future through the power of hope in that business. It is leadership confidence that improves the future; hope combined with action can positively impact culture, improve financial performance, and resolve organizational issues as well as virtually any other business problem.

Hope Serves Others

HOPE TRANSFORMS BOTH the person who hopes and the people who hope serves. People who are actively engaged in serving others often report feeling a tinge of guilt for benefitting from that service even more than those who are being served. It is a universal axiom that when we get out of ourselves and into the lives of others, everyone benefits. Barak Obama said it this way: "The best way to not feel hopeless is to get up and do something. Don't wait for good things to happen to you. If you go out and make some good things happen, you will fill the world with hope; you will fill yourself with hope."

Hope serves others by giving time and resources. Hope serves others by sharing experience and wisdom, and hope serves others by daring to believe that others can be hopeful. It is bold to believe that hope is something for everyone and something that can be given to others. When we look around the world, the news bombards us with the misery of mankind, and individuals seem to be more pessimistic than optimistic. It is our natural propensity to look for what is wrong rather than what is right. However, hope smashes through this paradigm and not only changes one's outlook but also serves others to make the world a better place!

The Golden Rule of leadership is that it is a privilege, not a right. Effective leaders serve others. Hope is the mechanism for this service. Kip Tindell, the co-founder of The Container Store, embraced a servant-leader tenure by focusing on how the Container Store could not only sell product in a tough retail environment but even serve far more than the customer. It is conscientious capitalism, summed up best by these words, "If you're lucky enough to be somebody's employer, you have a moral obligation to make sure your employees wake up and look forward to coming to work in the morning."

It has been well-documented and stated countless times that the best leaders are those who have a "servant mentality." Richard and Randy incorporate this mentality into every leadership role they assume; they believe that by serving others, either as a leader or as a person in their community, they can make a positive difference in their lives.

One of the most meaningful events in Randy's life, relative to hope serving others, is that of his daughter's cancer. As mentioned earlier, she has been battling pancreatic cancer for nine years, and hope has played a major role in this miracle. Nine years ago, she arrived home from the hospital with her newborn baby and what looked to be a death sentence within the next year. Within days of Randy's daughter's arrival home, her loving neighbor brought over purple pancreatic cancer wristbands — with the words "Hope, Courage & Faith" imprinted on them —to the family and to the entire neighborhood. This neighbor provided not only the family but everyone they knew with the hope that they could ignore the forecasted doom and beat the odds. Nine years later, Randy still wears his wristband as the best reminder that hope not only serves others but motivates others to serve.

As a servant leader, you constantly hope that, as you serve others, you will see their lives improve in numerous ways. In the business Randy led in Mexico, most of the employees were less than 20 years old, lived at home, and were poorly educated. He believed that by training them, increasing their confidence, and helping them to maintain their commitment to their families, he could serve others and instill the hope that they could rise to a level of success that they never dreamed was possible. Through his hope to instill allegiance to their business by serving their fundamental learning needs, he witnessed dramatic changes. Hope turned a raw street graffiti artist into a design leader and communications specialist. Hope transformed young people with less than eighth-grade educations, helping them to become group leaders and teachers to other teenage employees. Hope inspired a hard-working young leader to take a job as one of the first local Mexican nationals to become a plant manager. Hope not only serves others, but it also changes lives and, going forward, makes our civilization a better place for all!

— Story Two —

Real Life Application: Hope in Leadership

WHEN ONE LEADS with hope and makes hope the cornerstone of leadership, one changes lives, instills hope in others, and manifests miraculous results. Daniel McCollum has put hope in the cornerstone of his business, Torrent Consulting, which was founded in North Carolina, but now operates out of Guatemala. When we interviewed Mr. McCollum, we discovered that he views business as more than creating business and as a strategy for "raising up impact-driven leaders, who want to build a business to ultimately change lives."

McCollum is an interesting leader who served non-profits in various capacities through missions work and spent years in the corporate world, including a stint with Bank of America. But the realization that hope is a cornerstone came to him while doing mission work in Malawi. This is where he noticed that the local and foreign businesses were more engaged with the community than professionalized missions. It left an impact on him and the desire to start a business that would impact people.

When we talked to McCollum, who has had numerous stories in various media outlets recounting his amazing journey to success, he was taking a break from the ninety-percent tropical humidity in August to share his ideas on how hope is a cornerstone of great leadership and his goal of transforming community, one person at a time, to create a cadre of future leaders. He did so because he wanted us to hear about hope, transformation in Guatemala, and how the future of the country is being changed, one person at a time.

When Torrent reached 50 employees, McCollum set out to move the operations of his company to a place where his business could serve others. Torrent now has about 100 employees, 27 of which are in Guatemala. He has inspired hope among the hopeless. At the time we talked to him, waves of thousands of refugees were journeying from Guatemala to the United States, risking death in a dangerous journey on the slim hope that they somehow might be admitted to America when they show up at the border and might somehow escape the hopelessness of their present situation.

This is what motivates McCollum. He has the desire and the drive to serve within a community by inspiring hope among people in hopeless conditions. He instills hope where over half the population lives in poverty. With the right tools, the right training, and the right opportunities, the hopelessness of having a home can transform into the hope of creating a home — right there in Guatemala.

In the section of our book, focusing on hope as a strategy for leadership, we articulated five principles:

- Hope is a cornerstone of great leadership.
- Leaders inspire hope.
- Generational leadership is spanned by hope.
- Hope invites future leadership.
- Hope serves others.

The leadership McCollum has displayed is

servant leadership, a powerful form of leadership that, in this case, illustrates each of these five key points.

Leadership that brims with hope is a leadership that produces great results. Just speaking with him was inspirational. The reason? He had story after story of real hardship and pain, stories of real loss and sadness in a country plagued by political, economic, and human suffering. However, each of those stories ended with transformation through hope — transformation through business, with an investment in training unskilled workers from the most disadvantaged parts of the country. This has brought personal transformation to the employees and opportunities to the communities where they came from. By investing in hopeless people, and instilling them with hope, better things have come, despite the hardships of the past. One story he shared was of a woman who had suffered unimaginable violence and loss but now is working in technology and pursuing her degree at a great university in Guatemala. She is transforming the lives of others through business and hope for her community.

Clearly, McCollum is serving others. It is no

coincidence that his ideas about business come from a sense of mission and serving. By solving problems, his company is creating hope: the kind of hope that raises up future leaders.

Dramatic experiences like those of McCollum and his employees always inspire others and create a sense of wonder. How many of us would take our business to a place of need, with the goal of using our business to transform communities? It's a huge leap of faith and even flies in the face of business logic in many ways. But every business, no matter where it is located, has an opportunity to apply the five elements of hope in leadership right out their own front door.

Part III

Progression in Business Provides Hope

A S WE MOVE into the last segment of this book on hope, we now turn our focus to the role hope plays in building businesses, enabling employee success, driving business growth and performance, and the generational future of a business. We also share with you some practical and proven tools that you can use to ride the wave of hope to lasting success.

Progression is defined as the process of developing or moving gradually towards a more advanced state. In order to really think about a business progressing, think about a series of numbers that progress, such as 2, 4, 6, 8, 10, etc. When you think about progression within a business, it will look like this — a business concept with strategy development built on the conceptual plan and start-up and growth of a business, and, finally, business expansion. Thinking about that progression of a business from concept to expansion may be one of the single biggest sources of providing hope to a multitude of people. It is not just the entrepreneur or the family that are filled with this, though. Hope is extended by those who finance this venture. Hope is extended by the community leadership for the growth of jobs and tax base for the community. Hope is a real significant factor for all the local residents for whom this creates a job. Hope is at the heart of local suppliers to this business, who see their own businesses' growth. This hope for a better future, a stronger community and more jobs only becomes magnified when and if the business expands.

If there was not this powerful thing called hope, why would any person or business ever take the risk to progress?

In addition to the concept of hope driving business progression, business progression drives hope as well. New businesses with new and better jobs help individuals look beyond the challenges of today and develop hope for a better tomorrow. Think about the period of technological evolution that all of us are living in today. The future of technology appears to be even stronger than the present or past, but that, too, is driven by hope. Hope is looking forward to the future, and a hopeful outlook enables people to see beyond today's challenges to tomorrow's solutions.

Hope transformed personal transportation from the horse & carriage to the automobiles, and the future promises that hope will drive autonomous vehicles. Hope drove serums that eliminated epidemics. Hope drove the technology to provide us with images of the inside of the human body, and hope will drive DNA testing, which will one day provide proactive solutions to diseases such as cancer. Hope is a genuine feeling of what is possible. As described by the few examples above, hope is much more than a dream or a wish. Hope drives change, and change drives hope! I hope for my daughter to beat pancreatic cancer, and that hope has driven us to try new medicines, overcome our discouragement at times, and hold on to the belief that she can beat this. However, at the same time, I hope for a future cure that will prevent my grandchildren from having this disease. That hope drives my involvement in fundraising to support clinical trials that will achieve that goal.

It is our strong belief that hope is the cornerstone of our lives. If you are seeking employment, you must hope that the progression of business in the community will provide that suitable job one desires. If you are a business developer who is grossly strapped for funds to expand, you must believe that you can find that support from a place that has that hope of progress. Think about how life would be for any of us in the business world without hope. Do you know the old business saying that "Hope is not a business strategy"? We agree that hope alone is not a strategy, but hope, combined with various other goals and intentions, is truly what drives business success and progression. Libby Gill, an executive coach and leadership speaker, said, "I believe hope is the only thing we can <u>never</u> afford to be *<u>without</u>* and the jet fuel for the journey of work and life."

However, on the other side of the hope coin, one of the biggest "hope killers" is the failure to recognize advancement along the pathway to progress. Warning: This is a mind trap often fueled by corporate training and motivational posters that stress goal-setting rather than intention setting. The result? When goals are set as all-or-nothing, our thinking process often hides the progress we have made along the way towards our goal. Too often, the focus is on the future without regard to the starting point and the incremental progress towards the goal. Unfortunately, this technique all too often leads to frustration and discouragement and is one of the top hope killers!

It kills hope by developing the theme that, "Until I reach my goal, I haven't achieved anything yet." The reason this is a mind trap is that incremental development is, in fact, progress, but with all of one's focus on the goal, the present progress is often overlooked. Progress teaches us lessons and helps us define our goals and do today what really matters today. Goal setting is only about the future, but intention setting is about today. We encourage intention setting because it fosters progress. An intention can be set right now, and an intention can be attained right now.

What intentions do you need to set for yourself to create progress? The intention to be dedicated? The intention to share product benefits with potential customers? The intention to build relationships for the long-term? Do you see the difference? I can be ethical (an intention) right now, even if I have not yet reached the goal of selling 1000 widgets to customers who will truly benefit from them.

By clearly marking your starting point with intention setting, you double the likelihood of creating hope and using it as a strategy. When you find yourself saying, "Drat, I have not yet reached the goal!", this hopelessness is coming from the mind trap that did not remember the starting point. It may be true that the goal might not yet be reached; but for example, one year ago, the product did not even exist. One year ago, the team did not yet exist; one year ago, the message was unrefined. But today, there has been progress. Maybe everything has not yet been accomplished, but by using intention to make 20% progress, or 40% progress or 60 % progress towards a goal creates hope. It provides hope that the best is yet to come, it provides hope for the future, and it is the catalyst for lasting transformation.

Hope Drives Change

RICHARD RECALLS WHEN he felt hopeless in a dead-end job — well, at least a job without much upward mobility. He was 29 and had asked the CEO how she became the boss. As he listened to her story of rising to the top, he noted how her experience and education were far different than his. He was working as a family therapist in an adolescent treatment program and was barely making enough to cover his cost of living, including student loan payment and a car payment. The only management job between him and the CEO was that of clinical director. However, even the clinical director didn't make much more. In the world of clinical care, fancy titles often come without big raises. He had two small children at the time and begun questioning his career choice.

The following week, Richard attended a mandatory training session for mental health professionals. Every year, licensed psychother-apists are required to have a certain number of continuing education hours to remain licensed. He listened to the boring instructor drone on about abstract ideas and applications that really were not practical to the clients he was seeing in inpatient care. In a moment of boredom, he counted the number of people attending this mandatory event. There were 108 people in the room. Each of them had paid $100 to be there. That equates to $10,800.

It was at that moment that he had an epiphany. Even though he was young, he knew as much as the keynote speaker. Richard loved seeing clients, reading journals, and looking for applications of research to real life. More importantly, he was far less boring than this expert up on the stage was. He went back to the CEO that day and turned in his notice. That is how he started his business. It really was that simple. Hope drove a change. He remembers driving home from that class, counting an imaginary $10,000 in his mind, AND seeing smiles on the faces of happy participants rather than bored chair-takers. That was almost 30 years ago, and he still runs the continuing education company he started. He began with very little capital for some postcard advertisements with the catchy slogan, "Just say 'NO!' to Boring Workshops!" and a whole lot of hope.

Hope drives changes in individuals, communities, and companies. Some companies have even recognized the transformational value of making hope a central value in their company culture. Torrent Consulting, a Salesforce consultancy firm in North Carolina, starts by hiring people who care about hope, and the reason is simple: People who hope, show a strong desire to make the future better than the present. The CEO, Daniel McCollum, told us, "Business is more than creating economic opportunity. It raises up impact-driven leaders, who want to build a business to change lives."

Hope drives change by activating motivation, which leads to inspired action, and provides the enthusiasm for big changes to take place. The book, titled "Who Moved my Cheese", is often used to help employees who dread change to begin to see change in a more favorable light. Companies spend billions of dollars each year, attempting to get employees' acceptance and "buy-in" for change. Change, though, usually remains in the domain of dread and despair despite these efforts. What is missing? It is not another explanatory meeting, nor is it another lesson in change being the normal state of the business. Rather, what is often missing is the secret sauce: Hope!

One of the craziest stories in the business world is when Alan Mulally, the man credited with turning around a hopeless Ford Motor Company in 2008, instilled hope in his dealers by ditching the teleprompter and then walked out to the stage and asked the corporate employees to stand and yell, "I love you" to the 4000 dealers who attended the annual dealer meeting. Mulally explained, "Act like you mean it, and it will become a self-fulfilling prophecy." We could easily fill another book studying the relationship between love and hope but, suffice it to say, being valued is a universal pathway to feeling hope. Mulally knew this, and he knew how to create a partnership between the corporate Dearborn staff and the dealers spread all across the company; they are the ones who really sell cars. The amazing result of this hope was an unmatched period of prosperity for Ford, which was based entirely on the recognition that hope creates change.

Hope drives changes to the culture of a company, which result in a company's increased financial success. The result of this success in believing in hope, in turn, creates more hope. This is the corporate culture that should be shared in a company's vision. These days, creating and focusing on goals or objectives for a business is simply not enough. One must have and instill hope. Hope enables people to propose a better way of doing things. Hope enables people to further their education and to drive the qualifications for career growth. Hope enables the community leadership to create tax incentives to create jobs. In each of these instances, hope is the clear motivating factor that each person believes will drive change. There is no guarantee of those changes, but hope can be the motivating factor that instills that belief that these changes not only can but <u>will happen</u>!

Why do we have change? Please take a moment and really think about it. Wouldn't our personal and business lives be much simpler without the burden of change? You are reading this book because you already know the answer to this question. We have to change in all aspects of our lives to not just thrive but survive! Change is something that any individual can only do themselves. As Randy has stated many times before, that change is the only constant in life if you want personal growth and achievement. In order to facilitate change, we need a vision or dream of a better job, family, community, or numerous other things to move forward with the changes required. Hope is that critical attribute that lifts our minds, our eyes, and heart to that future place following change. With hope as that facilitator, we see that new opportunity, new paths to improvement, and an improved future for the individual as well as the business. A business that instills hope in its associates that there is a better way, new career paths, security for their future and less threat in change is a business with a strong future and a committed workforce!

When people are hopeful, they look to the future and see opportunity in change. With all that said, please note that hope is not a blind cure-all for change either personally or professionally. Hope is a catalyst to drive change, but it must be accompanied by strong leadership, good strategic thinking, and excellent execution. Failure on any of these fronts can kill hope briefly, but success in these areas can revive hope and create exciting change. Randy knows and understands this because that was his role in three different CEO assignments in failed businesses. He revived hope, facilitated change, and had a ton of fun with lots of great people!

Hope Must Be Your Corporate Culture

L EADERS WHO EMBRACE the value of hope produce a culture of hope. A hopeful corporate culture is more than a nice place to work; it is a place where employees thrive, and customers feel satisfied. Hope produces behaviors that transform results. In other words, if you want your company to prosper, then hope must be the cornerstone of that culture.

The common denominator in failing businesses is hopelessness, and its despair can be seen in every aspect of corporate culture. On the other hand, the common denominator in successful businesses is a vibrant corporate culture — and that is always founded on hope. For example: You have been to a business with a rotten culture. You walked in and walked out knowing that the axiom "a fish rots from the head down" was at work in every level from management down to the clerk who helped you. You have also been to the opposite, a business where you were greeted with a smile, and even if a solution was not provided or a purchase was not made, you wanted to refer this business to others because it was just a wonderful place to be.

Inspiring and cultivating hope in your company culture begins with one person — one person who makes the decision to act on hope and embrace its power. This is done by affirming the power of I Am. RJ Banks, who wrote a magnificent little book called *The Power of I Am, and the Law of Attraction* says, "Focus equals fuel." For you to be the one who begins embracing hope, your focus must be on what is hopeful. Ask yourself, "What possibilities exist?" rather than, "What are our limitations?" Ask yourself, "What is working?" rather than, "What in this company is broken?" The results will amaze you. As you focus on those things that bring hope, hope will become your fuel.

Corporate culture is not created in a boardroom. It is something that comes from knowing the hopes, the dreams, and the desires of both employees and customers and even the broader community. When a company works towards empowering people with hope, it resonates on every level and becomes more than a slogan or cliché — it becomes a powerful reality.

Jeff Applegate is the CEO of Texas Injection Molding. He walks the floor and talks to his employees; he knows what their needs are, as well as what and why they go to work. When the devastating hurricane hit Houston and closed the city and displaced residents, he knew how to bring together competitors in the plastics molding business to meet the specific needs of hurricane survivors by buying clothing for children, sheets for the bed, and helping one-on-one.

A culture that is built on hope is a culture that is sustainable. Hope creates energy. It creates vibrancy; it creates appreciation and is the cornerstone of lasting success.

The title of this chapter is a fairly bold statement. There are likely hundreds of words other than hope that can be used as the "<u>must</u>" for a successful corporate culture. In today's world, we hear a lot of focus on corporate culture, with focal points including inclusiveness, transparency, eco-friendliness, and diversity, and as you know,

Randy Dobbs & Dr. Richard K. Nongard

that list goes on and on. So, are those objectives for a corporate culture less important than hope? It wouldn't be fair to say they were less important, in fact, to some groups of employees, they are extremely important. This importance is relative to their choice of employment and overall job or business satisfaction. With that said, we say to most employees that none of those objectives, in and of themselves, are more important as a culture to the majority than the culture of hope. We have found that most employees' livelihoods depend on receiving their compensation at their planned pay period. Beyond that, they hope for increased compensation, better benefits, education for their children, good housing, and much more. Many people in this country love the fact that they belong to a corporation that supports and allows them to realize their hopes. Hope as a corporate culture not only allows but encourages those willing to work for it to pursue their hopes and dreams.

Randy shares a recent experience about a local business that, via its corporate culture, is instilling hope in some employees who really had <u>no hope</u>! In the words of Randy: "I recently purchased a new washer and dryer which were delivered to my house (on time, by the way) a few days later. The two young delivery agents were very hard-working, focused on the details, polite, clean-cut, and apparently very happy with their jobs. I love to engage with folks to learn more about their business environment. So, I told to them what a great job they were doing; everybody loves a sincere compliment. Then I asked how long they had worked for this company. They both replied that it was a relatively short timeframe, but it was the best job and company ever! I said, 'Wow! That is something. You guys work in the heat/cold, rain and have to do lots of heavy lifting all day. So, why is it the best job ever for you two?' They looked at each other, and then the driver, who I think quickly trusted me, said, 'It is because someone gave us hope again!' 'Really? How was that?' I said. They both confided that they were former addicts who were constantly in trouble, in jail and headed to an early grave. They heard about this program and, through a series of hard actions only they could hope and do, positioned themselves to be given a chance in this program."

We shared more about this in story one, but it is exciting to see how much a corporate culture can really do in today's world to drive real hope and change! Randy is continuing his relationship with these two young men to be another point of mentorship for them and help them as they live their hope every day. In addition, that same young driver sent Randy a text that said, "Once you are acquainted with hope, it is time to give hope back!" Hope is real!

Hope Serves Others

A S STATED EARLIER in this book, Richard and Randy strongly believe that the only true way to lead successfully over the course of a career is via "servant leadership". What do they mean by servant leadership? In simple terms, it means: "You are put in charge of an organization, and it is your responsibility to know and do what is necessary to support that organization's success." In other words, it is not their job to serve the desires of the CEO, but rather the CEO's job to serve and direct them to achieve the goals/objectives of the business. So, what this really means is that, as a leader, you place the needs and interests of your organization over your own needs or self-interest in the business. There are several key characteristics of servant leadership, and we will share them. However, to us, the most important characteristic found in servant leadership is authenticity. We find that being a real person with your organization genuinely wins them over. If you are honest, admit when you don't know, ask for their opinion, pay attention to all levels in the organization and actively listen, you have the mold in place for servant leadership.

We have found that servant leadership is the best and most successful way to lead. It's a leadership style that focuses on serving the hopes and needs of others such that one can secure their involvement in the resolution of various business problems. It is important to note that this servant leadership (driven by authenticity) is not a short-term process. It is every day! It is not an act but a way to believe. It can take months for the people in the organization to believe there is hope again, but they do want to hope and believe. Without hope, there is defeat, depression, and a continued downward spiral. As servant leaders, we facilitated hope, change, and some tremendous success stories about a renewed and hopeful organization.

Servant leadership is a theme we see throughout business, communities, and people. In common 12-step programs, such as Alcoholics Anonymous, newcomers start their recovery process by sticking around after the meetings to stack chairs, clean coffee cups, and help clean up the building. This is powerful advice based on the principle that when we get out of our own lives and into the lives of others through service, even simple service, we improve our own life and increase our abilities.

Many companies ask their employees to serve the community by being on volunteer boards and community committees and to come alongside the community through service. These companies know that the rewards of encouraging servant leadership and helping employees find opportunities to develop servant leadership will provide high dividends to their own company.

Hope that is developed in service to others is hope that strengthens people, leaders, communities, and businesses. It creates a lasting hope by getting out of our own lives and into the lives of others. It creates a lasting hope by creating belief in other people and something bigger, and it creates a lasting hope by tapping into the collective consciousness of a community. That community can be within or outside of a parent organization.

How effective is servant leadership? Under the guidance of former CEO Herb Kelleher,

Southwest Airlines has sustained profits through even the leanest of times, even as other airline companies declared bankruptcy. Southwest has one of the lowest rates of employee turnover, and Southwest has specifically credited servant leadership as the reason for this success.

The Container Store is a retail store that continues to thrive despite the lean times for retail outlets in the era of Amazon's online dominance. The secret? Kip Tindell, who is both the founder and the soon-to-retire CEO of the Container Store, has stressed the importance of serving employees, the community, and others over share-holder profits. What is amazing about this is that when a business focuses on what really matters, the financial results produce themselves. In the end, shareholders have been rewarded, and the company continues to thrive, with retail stores located in strip malls throughout the USA.

So, if you hope to improve your business, your organization's morale, your career, or your own financial rewards, please think first that these hopes are best achieved by serving others and their hopes. Serve others through active listening, commitment to employees' personal growth, integrity, empathy for other people's feelings, creating a sense of well-being for all, using persuasion versus authority, and creating visions that can be understood. These attributes of servant leadership have enabled the hope of others as well, beyond our wildest dreams.

Hope Drives Business Future

How is leadership measured in business? We think that leadership is measured in business by creating a lasting transformation, a transformation that outlasts the tenure of any individual leader. A core tenant in transformational leadership is the idea of creating a cadre of future leaders. This is accomplished by instilling hope. Hope drives a business's future. It drives the ability to take leadership to the next generation.

How exactly does hope drive the future of a business? When hope is the cornerstone of corporate culture, hope becomes the fuel that carries leadership into a new era. Hope activates vision, and hope becomes the inspiration to succeed. Robert Fulghum said, "Hope always triumphs over experience." The reason is simple: Experience is momentary, but hope is the bridge to the future. Experience can be forgotten, but hope becomes the DNA of any successful company.

Jonas Salk said, "Hope lies in dreams, in imagination, and in the courage of those who dare to make dreams into reality." Almost any company founded by a dreamer has been challenged by finding a successor who could carry on that dream. Hope is always the cornerstone of this successful transition. Founders hope for someone to carry on that dream, and successors hope to create a transition that builds on those dreams. Again, hope is the cornerstone.

There are three ways we can activate hope as a mechanism for driving business future. They are:

- Hope can be used to create bridges to the future.
- Hope is a foundation for sustaining change.
- Hope can be a roadmap for future decision making.

As a bridge, hope leads a business into the future. One simply cannot get from here to there in this world without bridges. Heck, you can't even get around any state without bridges. Oklahoma is nowhere near a large sea, but even in Oklahoma, bridges over creeks, rivers, and lakes are essential. Likewise, in business, there needs to be a bridge when technology changes, when economies change, and when consumer demands shift. Hope is the bridge that spans these huge challenges that businesses face. It is the bridge because hope is a strategy for decision-making, planning, and cultivating leaders.

Change is the natural state of business — everything changes. During periods of change, hope is the foundation, the anchor, the cornerstone that remains constant. Hope has a remarkable ability to be present no matter what the present circumstance. From hurricane-flooded Houston and Mr. Applegate waking up to a company in distress, to employees with real-world needs, and a community devastated, it was hope that remained.

Have you ever wondered, "What should I do in a business?" Have you questioned what the next step should be or how to go about taking new actions? Hope is the roadmap for all of these questions because hope is intuitive. It is subconscious, and when hope is cultivated as a foundation of corporate culture and personal leadership, it is automatic.

We cultivate hope as a catalyst for business future by dwelling on hope, by paying attention to it, and by sharing it. Develop a mindset of hope by living in the moment and knowing that whatever changes are taking place, hope is always present. Cultivate hope by looking for what is right and drawing on your own strengths rather than trying to fix the deficits. This is the approach of <u>Appreciative Inquiry</u> in business and <u>Positive Psychology</u> in personal development, and it is an approach that decades of research has shown to produce real results.

A fitting end to this book is to talk about hope driving the future. Hope does drive the future of businesses, but it also drives the future of everything. Hope, for all forms of business success, has driven so much change and new futures in our lifetime that it would be impossible to write about it all. That same hope drives businesses to find cures for today's incurable diseases, displace cars with individual air transportation, develop new and more healthy food sources, and just about anything else one can dream. Truly, the hopes and dreams of the businesspeople of tomorrow will drive more future change!

With all that said, why is it that we feel hope is so important to the future of a business? Business, like life, can be challenging, with various obstacles to success. Setting objectives for a business's future is simply not enough to ensure its future. Hope is that intangible motivator that pushes people not only to see but to identify solutions for the inevitable issues any business will face and creates, among many, the will and resolve to achieve future success. Hope drives others to see how the action of a few strong change agents can positively impact their organizations and follow their lead.

In the first 90 days of every business leadership job Randy had, it was his responsibility to define the business issues preventing a successful future and create a simple game plan that could provide hope for the collective future. Were his plans always 100% right? Absolutely not! He just had to be receptive enough to know the general issues and create a straightforward plan that would begin to instill hope again, not just in the business's future but the employee's future as well.

As we close this book and all of our thoughts on hope, let us state again that hope is the cornerstone of our lives and our future.

"We must accept finite disappointment, but never lose infinite hope."

— Story Three —

Real Life Application: Hope in the Real World

T HEIR SCHOOL MOTTO: "Work Hard. Go to College. Change the World!"

Today, Democracy Prep is a successful charter school experiment that started from a single Harlem school project in 1999. It now boasts over 23 campuses nationwide. Adam Johnson became the Executive Director of the new Las Vegas campus in 2017 when Democracy Prep merged with the Agassi charter school.

The campus was built by the Andre Agassi Foundation with hopes of transforming a disadvantaged community with feelings of marginalization amongst its youth and some of the lowest high school graduation rates and college acceptance rates in Nevada. Despite backing and donations from Agassi and his powerful friends, including Carlos Santana, students displayed little hope of ever catching up and becoming competitive in today's world.

Like many leaders to take over a challenging situation, hope was really all he had. When you meet Johnson, you can't help but notice his sharp intellect and his sincere belief that any child, from any disadvantage, cannot only get as far as their old man got (to harken the lyrics of Billy Joel's song Allentown) but can exceed their parents success, and excel wildly beyond what a communities expectation is.

The five principles of hope in the real world that we articulate in this book are clearly evident in the ongoing leadership of Mr. Johnson and the work of Democracy Prep at the Andre Agassi campus. These five aspects of hope are:

- Progression in business provides hope.
- Hope drives change.
- Hope must be your corporate culture.
- Hope serves others.
- Hope drives the future of a business.

As Mr. Johnson assumed his new role, it was evident that it was time to drive change in order for Democracy Prep to achieve the lofty goal that it established in 2004. By establishing new education objectives, it was his hope for the school to provide a path of progression to show how hope lives for all involved.

His infectious hope for a senior class that all go to college was, and is, a hope that needs to be embraced by faculty, parents, and students alike. As those hopes were developed and understood by all, it required change. Some faculty embraced it with zeal while others left. Parents learned that college hopes for their children meant changes in study habits and commitment to the process. Students, while not hoping for longer days and additional homework, realized this focused effort on their behalf was the key to unlocking unlimited potential. Mr. Johnson's hopes are not just driving but facilitating change.

Anyone visiting the campus in Las Vegas would agree that it has long been a culture based on hope. In fact, one of the first quotes you see on the wall when entering is *"With education, there is hope."* There are also many other inspirational signs, posters, and banners in the school that speak of a culture of hope. At Democracy Prep, the culture is best measured by the results. In 2018,

26 seniors graduated, and 25 entered colleges that fall. Their hopes for the future really exhibit that the hope is not only a cornerstone of their culture but embedded in every thought.

Believing in servant leadership, we have to say that Democracy Prep is very fortunate to have Mr. Johnson as their leader. As we walked in the inspiring halls of the facility during our visit, Adam spoke with every student and member of the faculty that we passed. He knew them by name. He introduced us to faculty and had a story to tell about each contribution. It is clear that he understands that real hope is found in serving others. His hope is not to lose third and fourth-graders when the workload increases. He hopes to fill his ninth-grade class to a bigger number in the fall by spreading the objective hopes of college for all graduating seniors. Mr. Johnson is a tireless optimist (he said his wife called him Pollyanna when facing problems) who knows hope only survives by serving others.

Lastly, we spoke in the section of hope driving business future. Mr. Johnson, like all of us, knows nothing is forever. His most amazing hope to me was expressed in an almost off-the-cuff statement.

He said, "I hope that, with all that we are doing from a culture and operating process, there is now a child on the playground who one day will have my job!" Hope can't be sustained without the future leaders of hope. Hope serves the now and prepares the school for sustainability in the future.

One of the most basic of all-American values is the next generation should get a shot to make it at least as far as their parents got. But real-world demographic changes, especially since the last recession, have challenged the idea that this generation has that opportunity. Politicians will debate the policies that they believe will provide solutions, but Mr. Adam Johnson, the Executive Director at Democracy Prep Andre Agassi campus in Las Vegas, is not waiting for future solutions, he is leading his school with hope, and it's students are graduating one at a time, making real-world contributions.

Conclusion

HOPE DRIVES REAL life changes, business success/growth, and is at the center of servant leadership. This would be a world that was much more like the nightly news, if not for hope. This would be a world of less technology and tougher lifestyles if not for hope!

We would like you to know that our biggest hope was not that you would buy this book but that reading it would guide you to focus your day-to-day actions on goals fueled by the power of hope.

We do truly hope that you are now a believer in hope! Hope changed the lives of both these authors, and it continues to do so today! Thank you for reading our views on hope, and we hope for the very best for all of you.

Please visit www.RealHopeBook.com for free resources that can help you make the contents of this book a part of your leadership, your business and your real life.

Made in the USA
Lexington, KY
10 December 2019